BAKSHEESH

(Turkish or Persian: something
given, a gratuity, a tip)

Also by Karen Herseth Wee

"Aubergine," *Anthology of New American Verse*, The American Poetry Press, vol. 1, Atlanta, Georgia, 1974.

"Of Girls and Ropes and Swings," *Sing Heavenly Muse*, ed. S. Martinson, Minneapolis, MN, 1978.

"Shampoo," *Studio One*, St. Benedict's College publication, St. Joseph, MN 1978.

"Love Poem for the Nuclear Age," *Iowa Woman*, vol. 4, #3, summer, 1983.

"Cochineal Mask,"*The Inkling Selection*, an anthology, ed. John Hall, Inkling Productions Inc., Alexandria, MN 1984.

"Small Town Commencement 1984," *The Northfield News*, Northfield, MN, June 14, 1984.

"Eleven Ways of Looking at a Loon," *The Rag Mag*, ed. Voldseth Goodhue, MN, spring, 1984.

Absorb the Colors, anthol.,eds. Voldseth & Herseth Wee, Heywood Press, 1984.

A Rich Salt Place, anthol.,eds. Zelle, Easter, Gery, Heywood Press, 1986.

Before Language, Northfield Women Poets' Chapbook Series, Heywood Press, 1992.

The Book of Hearts, Black Hat Press, 1993. Nominee in poetry for MN Book Arts Award, '94.

KAREN HERSETH WEE

BAKSHEESH

THE BLACK HAT PRESS
GOODHUE, MINNESOTA 55027

Dedicated to my compatriot travellers,
in this world and the next...

CONTENTS

(The Poems)

Baksheesh

A Journey

In New York
an old man leans
against a skyscraper's
ground floor window
and stares up
into the giant mouth
of a beautiful billboard
woman Her red upper
lip looms high
above his head
On tip-toe he stands
to kiss the pane
mutters into
the chilly air
Behind him
another
shuffles past
She pulls a cart
piled
with the pieces
of her life
Later after theater
we eat chunks
of cheesecake
in a sidewalk cafe
and watch a long
black limo slide by
Two svelte women
stare out
from it

After New York City sights and cheesecake, the blue United Nations flag still flying in my mind, we fly to Rome. At nineteen, bare-armed at the Sistine Chapel, I was kept outside on the steps and left Europe without a glimpse of Raphael or Michael-angelo. Today at the fountain of Trevi, a coin tossed over my shoulder years ago shines in the dark of my memory. David runs in the Circus Maximus, and leather still holds Italians together.

In Rome
it poured rain
Lightning and thunder
came in the same instant
Still we ran
-all thirty-four of us-
for blocks
water sheeting
off our eyeballs
Bernini statues
on the Tiber bridge
stared through the rain
without corneas
stone togas soaked
Finally seated for the audience
our clothes refused
to dry   stuck
to our skins
crept into crevices

Karen Herseth Wee

For three hours in six
languages the pope spoke
about something dark
in Genesis   sin   I think
One of us touched him
At that moment under
the pope's nose
an unknown man
felt up one
of our women

Bus to Pompeii
Guitar music
like lava
slides
down the Spanish
steps
stops our students
in their tracks
holds them
and in the morning
as Italy awakes
and rolls past
our bus window
they sleep
through the castle
of Monte Cristo
on the left

On the right
two men pick grain
by hand outside
the glass
of the students'
sleeping minds

as heavy woman
kneels in a field
She lifts
cabbages
like childrens' heads
and puts them on a cart
that rolls away
She does not
look up
as our bus
speeds by

In Cairo, the heat in the Egyptian museum almost
melts stone, and the gold in Tutankhamen's tomb
seems as though it might rub off on our fingers. We
could take some to Ozymandius, the pharaoh on his
back at Memphis, make him sit up and notice that
his city has disappeared from around him; only a
small sphinx remains on guard.

In Cairo
looking down
on nothing I know*
my eyes follow the Nile
From this distance
I cannot see
that it is dirty
sludge almost   and slow
At night the city lights
like predators' eyes

Karen Herseth Wee

crowd the river
fall back or
s t r e t c h
up invisible alleys
digging imagined claws in
The lights blink on off on off on

I turn from the window
stare at my strange room
which also winks at the river
if anyone were out
there to notice
No one is... no one knows
where I am
that I fled recently to Cairo
in search of a time and place
to live intensely
in the moment
and not know
the lay of the land
like I do in Dakota

(lines 2 and 3 from <u>Alma</u> by Linda Gregg)

Islamic Cairo is crammed into a day of stooping,

stooping, putting my shoes in and out of canvas booties

at mosques. A British military man gone Egyptian,

Gayer-Anderson, left his house, bed, photographs,

to Cairo and to our imaginings. We wander through it

amazed, and later board a bus for Alexandria.

Mezzuin in minarets
echo Mohammad's call
across Cairo   Luxor
Alexandria   the deserts
and villages
I sit at the entrance
of a catacomb
listening for the sound
a leaf makes
as it drops into my lap
from an unknown tree

I do not go down like the others
I know something
of the underworld--
that deep down
Greek and Egyptian
blend in the dress of Anubis
as guards the underworld
I stay in the sun
and trace the leaf spine
with my forefinger
imagining Muhammad
Cleopatra, Antony
Saint Anthony--the first monk ever
Think in wonder of a lighthouse
burning on-coming enemy ships
by glass and the sun
Think of the centuries
of flotsam
in the Suez
at El-Alamein
Giza and
streaming
in Cairo streets

Karen Herseth Wee

Sand, sand as far as the eye can see, and at its
edge, the color aquamarine--water pure enough to
heal WWII, drown the Desert Fox, or rebaptize all
those boys who fell here on my sister's birthday in
1942.

The Mediterranean
an immense turquoise
tossed on white sand
its veins the black robes
of Bedouin women bathing

We defy the ghosts, bury Allison in the sand near
El-Alamein, give her paws like the sphinx. Her
lively eyes smile out as the students raise up sand
pyramids around her. A Welshman in work togs
hurries by, tells us oil wells soon will appear on this
beach, hates to think it, all that pooling black gold
in the hollows of the sand... and greed. A huge wave
washes over the girl-sphinx, she and the pyramids
are gone. We hurry back to Cairo, to our hotel, to its
welcome familiarities. We arrive just as the
khamasin blows in off the desert, wiping out our trail
behind us.

Eight stories up
in El Nil Hotel
a balcony view
of the Nile
Cairo the color
of rich sand
burnished
with bartered
piasters and pounds
compounded
on the black market
A sharp rap on the door
Mamoud slips in
Rolls of bills soon
quicken in his
lightning hands
Each day a maid
changes our sheets
but years of dirt
lie in the corners
of the room--
a small refrigerator
growls on the end
of its bare-wire cord
At breakfast
a red juice crushed
from flowers
tea with lemon
hard toast
the ubiquitous
strawberry
jam on croissants
the hairs in them
We never look
behind any doors

Karen Herseth Wee

Next Luxor, and the valley of Egyptian kings and
queens; home of our friend, Samiha, and of pharaohs.
We come by train, rocked awake to a dusty, golden,
rural world along the Nile, new sun and people rising
as dawn unwraps their lengths of cloth. Chickens
crow and scratch. Cats and dogs scuttle away. Heat
gathers strength from the edge where night retreats.
We hug water bottles to us, abandon them only by the
pool of the Isis Hotel.

In the Khan
Kalili Bazaar
greasy lamb stew
brews uneasily
A pigeon on my plate
curls its dead head back
along its naked body
beak buried in a slippery grain
It stares hollow-eyed
up from the nasty
red plastic plate
--a diabolic nest--
while a cat's eye watches us
through a crack in the table
It waits Our waiter waits
for *baksheesh*
I cannot eat pigeon
Cannot wait to go

Before settling into our rooms at the Isis Hotel,
we ride a *felucca* boat to Banana Island. Bunches of
the small fruited crescents hang in the trees; the
jungle breathes at our feet; from high in a tree a
*galebeya*ed man calls out picture, picture, picture.
Our cameras stop his body arcing from the trunk,
glinting in the jungle out over a long outdoor table,
laden like Thanksgiving dinner with veritable
courses of bananas. We peel back their skins, eat the
soft insides hungrily.

At Karnak Temple the evening sun bathes the
place rose--rose stone lotus pillar, rose stone papyrus,
our own bodies, rose. No photo nor memory can hold
it. Later like mummies, we sleep rapt and
transported.

Next day we take a boat north down the Nile for
hours. Like the British Victorians before us, we keep
a distance from the mud huts, the ancient river
rituals -- women and children washing pots and
themselves; chasing goats, each other, or a maverick
burro; small girls in red, bright yellow, and fuchsia,
following our boat with their sparkling eyes as their
mothers stand back swathed in black-veiled thought.
Their pushy sons stand at the edge of the water,
thrust small hips forward, expose their genitals,

then cartwheel and scream, laughing at us from the
edge of the slow-moving water. We do not avert our
eyes, but sweep on toward Dendara; do not
acknowledge to each other, the mote at the edge of
our eyes--the dark underbelly of a dead, bloated
waterbuffalo.

We return to Luxor down a road that was owned
by robbers just twenty years ago. We are told they
swept up out of ditches of tall sugar cane, fell on
innocent travellers, left them naked or hurt. Only
convoys guarded front and back were safe.

In the valley of the pharaohs, tombs like homes
sprawl under the sand, rich in red and blue
hieroglyphic story. We human scarabs escaping the
sun, scurry into as many shady holes as we can,
carrying water in our plastic urns. We can sense
mummies in shadow beside imagined gold chariots--
their invisible jewels gravely awaiting marauders.

Back at the American University Cairo, for four
hours at a time, Swanson the story-teller, rapid-fire
historian, wraps us in Egyptian history, rich as the
tombs -- he tells of fat King Said's friendship with
Ferdinand de Lesseps the Frenchman, and the

resulting Suez fiasco; digging the Suez trench, how
men like drowned beetles were caught in it.

Some nights a belly-dancer comes; fluid, full of
smiles and the motions of folk times in Egypt's better
days. Briefly we forget the sadness lurking behind
her eyes' fringe, forget our own shyness, and
sit for a while more loosely in our skins.

Finally we flee Egypt, and hours later, trudge up
the Via Dolorosa in Jerusalem, through the Lion's
Gate to *Ecce Homo* hospice and healthy food,
tomatoes--fresh-cut tomatoes--soup, ice cream.

Over Jerusalem
like light off jet plane wings
ancient Islamic calls
glint from the minarets
to clash in the sun
streaming down on the Old City
They meet a Jewish wail
head-on at the Western Wall
Neither can drown out
the clamor of Christian bells

Karen Herseth Wee

We reach the craggy Israeli countryside st ing
under urban sprawl; stretch our challenge
imaginations like a loincloth, over th
to rural times, to John the baptist in
the Israeli wilderness. We fin k no
milk; kahki-colored soldi ywhere.

We wind nort o the Sea of
Galilee. From we can view the Golan
Heights, h oughing in olive branches
and the bar hen we visit the small ruin of
Capernaum.

So many old stones rolled aside
Long ago on so many mornings
the women leaving
the tiny rooms
of this city
So big their news
Further south
Mary fetches water
at Jacob's well...
her mouth suddenly
goes bone dry

We are famished, and feed on Peter's fish, then
spin south to Qumran where a shepherd found Isaiah
wound in the Dead Sea Scrolls. Further on, it is
extremely hot on the summit of Masada, also later in
Jericho. Ghosts of old antagonisms appear among us,
a heavy taste of sand, homesickness, and isolation
coats my tongue -- I hardly want to leave the bus.

Bombay
could have been home
or Jerusalem
I could carry guns
along the barbed fence
in the Golan
or wear tatooed numbers
on the soft inside of my arm
Instead this small
American blue book
number 070570511
graces my name

and allows me to fly back to the Cairo airport, then
on to Bahrain Island in the bombing gulf, and to
Bombay in twenty hours! Our longest journey-leg.

Karen Herseth Wee

In the third world
water is better than gold
So rare
you taste it in sleep
slosh it on the tongue
push it out through
the gaps of your teeth
dribble it over dry lips
to the chin
It slides smoothly
down throats inside or out
even when putrid
even when the diarrhea comes

Women walk
miles for water
hoist it precariously
on to their heads--
containers of brass
copper clay
Then trudge home
the weight of it
pushing their feet
deep in the dust --
pottery women
their remarkable
breakable flesh
carrying water
rarer than gold

In Bombay we are rescued; two women lift us from

the streets -- dour Mrs. Wray of the Methodist home,

who feeds and houses us, and the glorious Kalpana

Ashar, who takes us into her confidence as she does

through the streets of Bombay, to Gandhi's spinning
wheel, or to the government buildings; then later, at
the Methodist home she reads our palms. Like an
angel visiting us, she returns a second night... we do
not want to let go of her hand.

At Mother's Teresa's center, Walt Disney murals
coat the walls, lost children lie abed. Our students'
hearts cry out--they try to help. At a primary
school, small children sing because we're there. Later
we get invited into a Muslim tenement -- someone's
tiny home, each meager room scrunching people
without work and with little hope into corners.
When we leave, however, their children make joy of
us, follow us down the street as though we piped
them.

At four o'clock a.m. in the Bombay airport, Dan
and Betty Palm, colleagues from school back in
Minnesota, materialize in thin air... they hand-
deliver a letter for our daughter from her friend in
China. We join up with them, go on to Bangalore and
the garden-idyll, the Ecumenical Christian Center.

Here in the trees, real monkeys play and peek
over students' shoulders in the classroom. We stay on
all the paths, for an array of snakes--vipers, cobra,
python slide in the grass at night. It's hard to sleep;

Karen Herseth Wee

the dark too strange to know, the mosquito netting
much like a shroud. Security guards snake through
the compound after dark, their wooden sticks
thumping, their whistles shrill--sometimes far ,
sometimes close, just under our windows or across the
way--we seldom see them.

In the day, freer than before, still we're penned
by campus edges. Here we can wear shorts, and men
and women play together hard, game after game of
volleyball.

Then, India comes to us: a swami, a woman
lawyer, a Sanskrit scholar, an untouchable-- each
devoted to their cause, and this land. *Vigil India*
women from distant Indian states, here to learn street
theater, later return home to teach their villages
what they've learned about clean water, health, and
education, the danger in their gutters -- rats, disease.

They like us, want to talk--with Ranjit as
interpreter, we sit in one huge circle, trying to know
each other better; end up laughing, dancing. They
spirit Carol home to learn from her the chicken
dance!

Ranjit

dark man
of light
wise
and one
with India
A power
in his gentleness
and face
His fingers know
the ache of bone
His eyes
the soul's

Gita

his special friend
The saree
we ask her
Is it not hot
constricting
so much cloth
dangling down
She laughs
deep in her ample belly
no no nooooo
her bobbed
black hair dances

Peering out the windows, we bus further south,
covering crowded Indian miles . In Cochin we see the
church where Vasco da Gama once lay buried till
Portugal insisted his body return home.

Karen Herseth Wee

Everywhere Oriental fishing nets dip their
graceful, hand-made, wooden frames into the water
and derrick-like, simply lift with weights of stone,
nets full of tiny, silver, struggling fishes.

A mosaic green: jungle, rice paddy, jungle, rice
paddy, jungle, creates the country--everywhere
people working, bending, working. Along the
highway, breathing our bus exhaust, saried women
crouch; they crack gravel off of stones, chip by meager
chip, making India's roads by hand.

Muslim women
peer silently
from black
homespun caves of cloth
into the tropical fluttering
landscape of lemon, lime
orchid, and tangerine sarees

In our Trivandrum hotel, a squalid, rat-infested
place where water runs down the walls of our room,
David and I dispel our worries about his allergies,
with candles and some tea, and gratefully seek next
day Kovalum beach. We watch from far off as our
students, quick into the water and pounding surf, do
not notice all the bodies scurrying toward them over

the sand till they are surrounded; the naked and the
clothed, not quite scared--all is sacred when so
little's known.

Cape Comorin, the furthest south we go, the tip
of India where three seas crash in meeting face to
face--the Indian Ocean, Arabian Sea, and Bengal
Bay swirl their waters underneath a seething
surface, blend in, as ethnic bloods could, but seldom
do. We fly back home to the ECC, as much a home as
home this far away can be!

On Halloween I went to the vegetable market
in Bangalore, India, for squash. She followed me
from the street to every food stall, and back out
to the street again. I could buy nothing. Her hands
were bound. Feet too. I cannot tell you now
the details, because I couldn't really look.
She had leprosy. On a cart in the street, her
husband held a daughter, waiting. I think it
was a daughter. They too had leprosy. I couldn't
really look. On the street they all followed me.
She, touching at my elbow with her bound hand.
I kept walking, not looking down, kept walking
with the friend, Dinshaw, with whom I'd come.

Karen Herseth Wee

He explained, do not give her anything. They make
enough money begging, some of them, to give their
children college educations. This one? This one , I
thought? We rounded them all up once, he said,
brought them to a clean place of three meals a day, a
cot, got them off the streets. They wouldn't stay, you
know, could make more money begging. Give her
nothing. This one? This one, I thought? as she
pleaded with her ragbound child, swaddled close,
her husband on the cart behind her. He'd been
turning its wooden wheels frantically with his
stumpy hands trying to catch up to us before the car
pulled away. I bought nothing. I gave nothing either.
We returned to Dinshaw's home, to its cool, marble,
tiled floors.

We leave the ECC reluctantly, the day is warm,
flowers bloom, and dogs, as usual, lope about their
doggy business. From center campus screams are heard
-- the ECC staff put out a challenge the night before
and volleyball resounds.

Twilight falls, the Festival of Lights begins, oil
wicks and sparklers gleam, small girls in elegant
sarees put glee into all our faces, both brown and
white. The entrance-way to the evening meal, a

chalk mosaic walk of pinks and blues and white, done
by hand all afternoon by the women in sarees, on
their knees. We eat chicken, rice, other foods I cannot
name, off wide banana leaves. David chews *pan* --
betel nuts and spice; he chews and chews and chews,
red saliva dribbles down his chin, to everyone's
delight!

A program follows, and exchange of gifts--
music, juggling, dance, and poetry. After a small
girl's serenade, come the *drums*--The Snake Dance
Daddies bring us to our feet. Their driving beat melts
our souls to one with sweat and still the beat goes on.
We leave reluctantly.

While we sleep our last sleep in the ECC, the
ghostly guards haunt the compound, blow extra-
shrill their whistles, drum the ground, and some-
where close a dog fight snarls, a disembodied radio
blares all night long from a nearby house we thought
was empty.

The House with No One in it--The Taj Mahal!--
Great and gorgeous tomb that sultan Shah Jahan built
in the 1600's for his favorite wife, who died birthing
her 14th child; his grief so deep, Jahan mourned in

Karen Herseth Wee

marble, red carnelian, lapis, agate tears, creating an
architectural, translucent dream.

We trace with our fingers twenty-four carnelian
stones in one small flower, multiplied over and over,
a symmetrical meaning found in what *isn't* here, like
in poetry; or beyond the edges of river where lies the
black and absent tomb the Shah had planned for
himself, but could not finish -- for his son had
imprisoned him. The bleak, dark foundations still
crumble down the centuries beside this river.

To Agra and back the road's unpaved, except
with every imaginable vehicle and burdened
creature: camels, bullocks and carts, tankers, people
afoot, on bikes, in rickshaws and cars, careening
lorries, we drive in a menagerie, while off the road in
the dark, lights flicker: wicks and lamps and eyes
that see us off to Kathmandu.

Mountains grand as any Taj Mahal await our
trekking souls. A lei of marigolds placed round my
neck, whisks me back in time to tiny streets, wool
vendors, people--walking crosses, their arms across a
frame of wood burdened by loads of hay or cloth or
shrubs or roofing metal. Monks, and nuns in saffron,
pad through these holy mountains--up, across, and

over with the ease of all downhill. Once at break-
fast as I stared down into a fabled street, an elephant
swayed by, great working beast, and I so close I could
have stepped out the window onto his back.

We trek up and out, past temples, past waving
paper prayers on trees, past saffron-gowned holy men
and women, past a Caucasian, prostrating himself
over and over before a Hindu god, his REI hiking
socks, the slides that shot his body forth and back,
again, again, again.

The days dole out over glorious mountain trails
and bouts of diarrhea, nights of cold. In the daytime
air the calls of children float after us: *namaste* hello
pen-give, hello *namaste* goodbye! We follow
Wangdowa and his lama cousin, trust they know the
way; they get us lost, Wangdowa too! The kitchen
crew has gone far ahead.

We wander in the terraced farmland close to
yokes of oxen pulling reined-in men behind single-
bladed plows; the people walking, walking, working;
children too, and most with running noses; older ones
with absent teeth behind such smiles as one would
think could melt the gold the women wear in their

noses, ears, and on their hands--golden hoops, these
rings, they wear their wealth.

We materialize from the dawn journey back in
the valley near the largest *stupa* in Nepal, our
hearts spinning like prayer wheels in the warm
Nepalese sun. We search for the Rum Doodle
restaurant and dig into its famous apple pie.

Another flight--to Bankok, Thailand, the
YMCA, and for supper, DQ ice cream. All get ill!

Our stomachs newly cleansed, we arrive in
Taipei, Taiwan, almost run--into Sophia Tung's
welcome arms. Sophia and Soochow, Helene and
Andy, Chinese students, they take our students home.
David and I huddle in our spare and welcome house,
eating tangerines, the largest suns of tangerines we've
ever seen. It is December of this trip.

Oracle bone writings
from the Shang dynasty
tell my love for you in yellow jade
In steamed-chestnut yellow jade, my love
the color for emperors
After writing
I rest my brush

in the hollow of your hip's mountain
feed you peaches
then wash with the kingfisher
who plummets from the sky

The days grow cold; carefully we inhabit the
spare apartment, our cold skins, but we are warmly
welcome. After hours of classroom study--Chinese
language, bronzes, jade, and Taipei women writers,
we head for landscape painting country--Shitou, and
a brush with *controlled* outdoor experience.

Here, hiking in the Taiwanese countryside the
people wear high heels, velvet, or three-piece suits.
We are confused. The guide explains to us that
needing country for the soul is new to the contempor-
ary urban Chinese; they have lost the art their
forbearers had just by nature, by experience. Here
trails are cement. And in the bamboo forest, we walk
past signs that document each natural event.

However, nothing can diminish the sacredness in
our bones as we walk silently through lime-green
bamboo.

Karen Herseth Wee

We step into a green glade
of slender poles
Here the wind plays bamboo
like a fine musician plays pipes
In the distance
green goes red
cascades
the mountain
in poinsettia
waterfalls

Anticipating Christmas, Dave and I buy cloisonne
book-markers for thirty-two, to mark this place in
time and journey, also cards, small oriental screens.
Again we count down days in fried-rice lunches near
Soochow and acrobatic leaps across a stage by child
opera stars. We see a romantic fantasy "The White
Serpent," one afternoon, which turns up later in a
four-hour lecture on porcelain at the National
Museum.

We bus downtown Taipei to meet a friend from
school, eat Peking duck with him--love the ritual,
the duck, and the hometown comfort of being with a
friend who speaks this language, can read the signs,
the lay of the land in this city.

Our down-island trip by train--we wake in
Hualien city, in a market with Sophia, choosing
fish. The Catholic hostel faces the Pacific, the
students sleep outdoors beneath the stars.

Next morning we travel through Toroko Gorge, on
a scar of highway dynamited through sheared-out
rock, (400 died building it), we're quiet, and search
for the cold water plunge that students from years ago
had told us to look for--it is gone. We learn it seeped

Karen Herseth Wee

into earthquake oblivion a year ago. Those baptisms
will exist now only on Global reunion photographs.

We cross Taiwan, go back to class, to lectures on
ancient Chinese bronzes, to translucent views in the
National Palace Museum of China's past in its
ancient porcelain; go to the night market -- our men
students drink snake blood there to prove virility (a
snake is cut and drained before their eyes). David
and I do not go... instead, at another market, we
purchase Christmas stocking gifts for our own three
children--a lapis goat, black onyx pig, and a tiger
made of jade, all knotted on three red strings.

The Grand Hotel--an exotic memory from years
ago, for Dave and I once stayed here, drank fresh-
squeezed orange juice late into the morning, loved.
We'd like to gift our children with an overnight this
Christmas, check the cost... and can't afford it. We
buy them *chops* instead, their own stone Chinese
signatures when pushed into hot red wax.

A few in our group fly off to the Pescadores,
where people lean into the wind and women bind
their faces up against the salt that flies--there they
break bread, eat fish with lepers, and follow
missionary Marjorie Bly on her rounds.

Back in Taipei, the rest of us enjoy a perfect
Christmas meal at Diedrichs'--ham and rolls, baked
potatoes, cheesecake--tastes of home that melt upon
our tongues beside a fire and a perfect Christmas fir.
(It had been flown in from Washington on the same
plane as the perfect giant fir in Taipei's downtown
marketplace.) We dream of home to background
Christmas music, the St. Olaf Choir.

Packed up and out, we fly like santas on a buying
binge, to Hong Kong island. And strew our YWCA
bedroom with thirty-four Nepalese woolen stockings,
awaiting stuffing by two blonde Santas--Kirsten and
Karen fill them with oranges, sweets, our bookmarks,
their own surprises.

For Christmas
Nalani
born in Hawaii
gives us roses
We give thanks
for her
and for all
the rest
of our
accompaniment

After one strange day in the PRC, "not the real
China," the Taiwanese tell us, our memories are
unreal--of Chekou and the model of an ancient

Karen Herseth Wee

ceramic horse and warrior, buried thousands of years
in a giant underground kiln. But very real are the
long, grey train stations, the grey barbed wire, the
long lines of unsmiling people; we try not to lose each
other.

A surprise note in our mailbox at the YWCA:
Buntrock relatives (my mother's family) I hadn't
known, invite us home to dinner on December twenty-
third, my parents' wedding day anniversary.
Wearing my baggy, Hong Kong rayon pants, I (and my
family) share a pew with them on Christmas Eve at
the Church of All Nations. I think how we could
have been here, shared this night, the pew, with
them, and never spoken to each other, not discovered
how closely we are related.

In the old days, all able-bodied Buntrocks
gathered each Christmas Eve at Grandma's house in
Columbia, South Dakota. So this is inevitable! Yet
all the connections relative to *this* moment had to be
just right... we await the Christmas miracle,
relatives together far from home.

In the morning thirty-four of us squish around our
hotel beds with gifts; later the students' phone calls
to family wing out over the Hong Kong mountains all
day long.

Hong Kong's buildings climb the sky. Outside our window, twenty stories up and just across, barefoot on the scaffolding, nimble painters in the rain paint a skyscraper Marlboro ad. When done they dismantle the scaffolding while still on it, bamboo pole by sacred bamboo pole, lower it rung by rung--they do not skip a rhythm, see us watching, wave and grin while hanging there. We hold our combined breath and snap them with our cameras.

We leave Hong Kong first class; don't know why, don't ask. For the next three hours, linen napkins line our laps, we eat salmon mousse with silver, and end the meal with a choice of port, gateau, or Irish Creme. So strange to eat this poshly, after where we've been and what we've seen.

At Shishakuin Kaikan, Kyoto, we receive the fastidious, gentle care of Tada *sensei* and the Buddhist monks. At night we sleep on *futons* on *tatami*; breakfast on our knees at low tables using black, Oriental lacquerware.

Karen Herseth Wee

On tatami
we are a far cry
from home
But what better
place to age
than in Japan
on 3 x 6 foot pieces
of woven straw
that never know
the soles of shoes
Like onion-paper screens
our skin slips
closer to the land
my heart to yours

On our first day, after a breakfast of toast and

tangerines, Kyoto city spreads itself before us, a

banquet--how to choose... Riononji Temple's vast Zen

rock-garden juts up five rocks from a sea of sand and

timlessness, a visual poem of what is and is not here.

Unbidden, haiku come.

(earthquake)
The windows rattle
The air in Japan goes cold
Even mountains shiver

Kiyomizu Shrine
juts out its wood and stubborn frame
over Kyoto

𝕹 ara, feudal city
Home of dhaibutsu Buddha
bronze butterflies, deer

Later at the Heien Shinto shrine, we stand in a
chilly wind on a covered bridge, reminded of being
here once before in another life. We see our younger
selves reflected in the lacquer mirrors we bought for
our small daughters years ago on *teapot lane*. Now
one is broken, the other gone. Many, many here...
they seem easy to replace.

We are lost one afternoon and surprise a cemetery
hiding bones just beyond a path we've walked almost
every day--a lost city of families, the marking stones
starkly upright, like *chops*, of Oriental signature.

𝕺 n this and every New Year's Day
the Japanese hurry past
sidewalk shops that sell
ceramic tea-sets and t-shirts
with kabuki face--hurry
toward Kiyomizu temple,
outnumbering the tourists
Black-robed men
sashed, on their wooden clogs
accompany butterfly women
in kimono, who trip
up the rough stone street
in too-small, satin thongs

Karen Herseth Wee

They mince toward
the wooden, winged temple
nesting in Kiyomizu mountain

When I brush past
wing-powder
clings to my clothes
Two gorgeous ones flutter
against the eye of our camera--
accepting its proposition
I watch carefully
wanting to crawl
out of my pale skin
My feelers twitch

    We celebrate the Rabbit Year (the rabbit,
David's running totem) in the New Year's Eve dark.
The Buddhist monks take us out behind the *kaikan*
trees. We line up, each get a turn, to flail a giant bell
a total of one hundred and eight times, scare away
the one hundred and eight sins with which we are
possessed.

The monks wear
purple and green satin robes
shining under a white moon
Tangerine offerings barely
rest on the altar
but float and glow--
suspended orbs
in an incense mist
that light the way
for a hundred and eight sins
fleeing the gonging bells

that cry in the night
of the Rabbit Year

By day, we study Japanese culture and how the
individual always sacrifices for the group. I read
Ariyoshi's The Doctor's Wife, how she and her
mother vie to be the doctor's guinea pigs, testing
potions at his whim, her awful death.

One night we're chased home by a political mob
or "gangster group," that screams loud harangues at us
on loudspeakers and chases us right up to the kaikan
door--the monks pull us in. Worried, ill at ease, they
call them "foolish groupa."

Professor Tada invites us to his home. We ride a
train, then walk a sidewalk maze of lanes through
Kyoto's suburb, past dark shrubbery, swinging gates,
finally through a particular gate, a particular door,
where a particular physician's daughter opens it and
invites us in. Tada *sensei's* wife. She serves us rice,
never sits, simply smiles and serves.

Karen Herseth Wee

I met her tall son
She gave us tangerines
when we left
So many small suns
to hold in our hands
like prayers
on the return train
She helps us forget
(and remember)
the great sun
we blanked out
that August, yet
I do not know her name

A few days later, Tada *sensei* takes us to

Hiroshima, his boyhood city.

I have stood in the spot of the falling bomb
The Enola Gay must have
seemed a giant bird
coming in that day
Or an angel   leaving

I stood in the cold of a January day
trying to imagine heat like that
Even the museum holding a man's shadow
burnt into cement steps
cannot tell of heat like that

A Japanese friend has brought me here
a man who was a boy in this city
He knew its alleys   the shortcuts
a good place to fish at the river
where to stand to wave long goodbyes
to his father   a Navy ship captain
who came and went from the harbour
and one day did not return

This man's mother has lived
fifty more years

Tada sensei tells us
he did not returned to Hiroshima
for many years
Today he stands with me
as I touch the stone-cold monument
dressed in bright origami cranes
the colors of blessings
He smiles wanly
tells me he remembers
two things
being hungry for food
being hungry for books
always hungry
I have met his sons
They are tall
I tell him how fine
and tall his sons are
Ask him if they had
a tall grandfather or mother
He says no   hesitates   no
just food
in their growing years

I have stood in the place of the falling bomb
with this man -- a poet
a writer   a Zen master
who translates English novels
into Japanese and who loves
the poems of Gary Snyder
Knowing him just this short while--
my blessing

Karen Herseth Wee

One day I hear the best lecture of my life.
Professor Abe, Japanese teacher of French, tells us of
bunraku puppets, as his grandmother told him. For
brief transitory moments, with Abe *sensei's* help, I
can step through the screen separating East from
West--perceive the elusive differences in our
thought, our ways.

He tells us how three men, who study all of their
lives, manipulate each puppet perfectly. To
manipulate a puppet head is a greater honor than an
arm; to move the arms better than the legs. He
explains how the Japanese are much influenced by
absence of space, presence of humidity, and great
population. So they create space between the self
and another -- they bow in greeting or farewell, they
peer into reflections, do not stare at the thing itself,
they have go-betweens--in business, in love, like
humidity eclipses the stars, or pools reflect the moon.

Puppets, he says, like kites (and some people),
are empty inside, they need energy, a go-between,
breath, which saves them, like a soul. They are the
shadows of humans, merely forms, like a reflected
moon, a shadow of the real. Their wish (like ours) is
to fly, defy gravity, like a soul winging toward

Karen Herseth Wee

heaven. A perfectly manipulated puppet flies like
an angel or a soul--it is the human form flying.

Abe *sensei*, my go-between, slips the East/West
screen aside, so briefly I understand. Knowing that it
will slide back again pushes tears to the surface of
my face. If Abe *sensei* looked closely into my eyes, he
would see himself reflected.

So, we go to Osaka to see bunraku theater;
afterwards I get lost.

The bunraku theater
empties itself
In the lav
old ladies push
Unwilling to push back
I am last
Hurry the water
over my hands
knowing the others wait
to catch the train
back to Kyoto

The language
around me buzzes
alive and indecipherable
Its oriental characters
leave the landscape
page of my mind
take awful voice and circle
me like birds of prey

I do not understand anything
rush down the balcony stairs to...

No One   No one's in sight
Could they have gone
without me? Has no one noticed?
Panic rises
like a dumb fur animal
in my throat
fur on my teeth
fur on the roof of my mouth
Unbelieving, I flee out the door
to the sidewalk
No one
Back in again   up
to the balcony
again down
Leave a scream hanging
on the ceiling
near a glass chandelier
I nearly shatter

Then a Japanese man
in a suit notices me--
asks "College? America?"
I nod
"Gone, gone train" he says
I grab at him
the voice escaping   not mine
"Forgot Forgot me Left me
Come Come please!"
I am bereft
Together we race
through underground corridors
toward an unseen train

Then David in the distance
feet off the ground
a puppet with no core
flying toward me
I own no breath
to fight down the fur

Karen Herseth Wee

that threatens to choke me
I bow
bow my thanks
hysterically
to the Japanese man
Something manipulates my head
my right arm
finally both legs
and I'm flying
toward David   found
and bound for home

The rhythm of lectures, learning, travel, visions,
touch, and dreams takes over. No spaces between the
lines for thought or poems. No time to pool
reflections. Over and over another presenter comes.

Human missiles, we shoot on the *Shinkansen*
bullet train through tunnels, over roofs, past the
crowded countryside. The grey buildings hug the
land.

Tada *sensei* takes us to Miyajima, carved
Miyajima dolls are everywhere. The tide is out on
this island, exposes the *torii* on a not-then-floating
Shinto shrine.

Later we follow Tada *sensei* (we would almost,
follow him anywhere) across a catwalk at Kobe Steel
where an immense molten slab careens by on rollers,

throws heat at our faces, then coils into a dociler form
at the end of the line. Cooling down, the molten red
becomes black, waiting to be put to use.

Like a rubberband, the schedule breaks and we
fly past Mount Fuji to a hostel in Tokyo, from which
we explore a little each day. Many of our students
are sick. One day we ride a train north to Nigata and
snow. Finally on January 15, the Japanese day of
"coming of age," David and I are alone in the Tokyo
museum.

We stop in the museum
on the second floor to stare
at watercolor sparrows
flitting in bamboo
No one else in all Tokyo
has chosen this spot
or this moment to come of age

Gold flecks in the second oriental screen
glint from sun behind pine
and gleam colder than the moon on bamboo

Across the hall
brush-strokes deft as Picasso's
create a street entertainer's monkey
putting smiles on a grandfather's face
Neither he nor the children never age

Later though, at the Meji shrine
the young samuri men do

Karen Herseth Wee

And women like ice sculptures
are caught on the path
melting

As we are caught
this perfect early morning
in a particular museum
one week before our return home
Come of age in time's moment
We appreciate sparrows
insouciant forever
in brush-stroked bamboo

    The mails bring a strange set of poems from Ranjit
in India. He is angry -- the East versus West stuff
scrawls from his hand. He says we are spoiled; says
we can't see beneath the surface of anything, in his
culture or any, and he's right. But we are here and
are trying.

𝔉or Ranjit--Questions

How many mountains
lie behind
the mountains I see
How many dreams
behind this one
Is Fuji really
just beyond clouds
You behind your poems

Tea ceremony, four hours of tea, teaches the value
of the moment, living *now*. We are told to give the
moment attention, respect it, ponder the uniqueness of
a particular person or thing, priceless or ordinary. Be
gracious as host or guest and know the obligations of
each, the rituals that remind. Use daily pieces and
priceless museum pieces equally in a daily way--
tranquility the goal.

On our last day in Japan, we revisit Sanju-
sangendo temple of the 1001 Buddhas. A Buddha is
not an image to worship, but rather an *awakened one*,
an image of the ideal. Can we be buddhas in our
lifetime? Live in the moment, contemplatively?
Know ourselves? Perceive reality, the thing itself,
no mere *transfer* of knowledge?

The screen is sliding, this journal becomes opaque.
A cloud descends on Mount Fuji, tea leaves settle to
the bottom of the pot that our students have give us.

Later, in Hawaii, Haleakala hides in the mist.
Soon we will come home .

Karen Herseth Wee